IN SEARCH (

The Caitlin Clark Biography

An Aspiration for Self- and Sport-Perfection

Bradford M. Neff

Table Of Contents

Introduction

Born on January 22, 2002, Caitlin Clark is one of the most well-known figures in American collegiate basketball. She is now a player for the Iowa Hawkeyes in the fierce Big Ten Conference.

Clark, an Iowa native from West Des Moines, attended Dowling Catholic High School, where she made a lasting impression on the basketball scene.

Having been named a McDonald's All-American, she cemented her place among the greatest players in her class and was ranked fourth by ESPN.

Clark's skill on the court was evident as soon as he joined the Iowa Hawkeyes. She raced to the top of the NCAA Division I scoring rankings her freshman year, winning All-American honors and receiving a great deal of praise.

Clark's outstanding play carried over into her sophomore year, when she accomplished the incredible distinction of being selected unanimously to the first team of All-America.

She made history by being the first female Division I player to lead the team in assists and points in a single season.

As Clark entered her junior season, her dominance only became stronger. She led Iowa to its first-ever berth in the national championship game and won every major national player of the year award. Her outstanding performance helped the team win another Division I assists championship and set new single-season marks for points and assists in the Big Ten.

Clark is about to start her senior year, and she doesn't seem to be slowing down. With her unmatched skill and commitment, she continues to rewrite the history of women's basketball by setting conference records in career points and assists.

Outside of the university setting, Clark has competed internationally and won three gold medals for the US team.

Her achievement of winning the Most Valuable Player award in the FIBA Under-19 Women's World Cup in 2021 is noteworthy as it further cemented her reputation as a basketball prodigy.

With a promising future ahead of her, Caitlin Clark is set to create history once again. It is generally anticipated that she will be selected first overall in the 2024 WNBA draft, solidifying her reputation as one of the greatest athletes in history.

The Making of a Basketball Prodigy

A basketball prodigy was quietly developing her skills amid the rolling plains of Iowa in the heart of the American Midwest, little knowing the seismic influence she would soon have on the sports world.

This is the tale of Caitlin Clark, a person whose name would go on to represent brilliance, tenacity, and the unflinching quest of greatness.

Having grown up in a household where athletics were not only a hobby but a way of life, Caitlin's journey started with a desire in her heart and a basketball in her hands.

She was dribbling, shooting, and envisioning herself on the big stage, enthralling people with her incredible talent, as soon as she could walk.

However, Caitlin's road to fame wasn't always clear-cut. She had her share of challenges and disappointments, just like any real victor.

However, it was because of these difficulties that she developed the perseverance and resolve that would enable her to reach previously unthinkable heights.

Caitlin's reputation grew along with her skill set. As word of her name spread throughout the state's arenas and gymnasiums, audiences gathered to see the enchantment of this teenage sensation.

Caitlin left a trail of broken records and shattered expectations in her wake as she etched her name into basketball history with each stunning show of agility and elegance.

There is a deeper story of passion, sacrifice, and steadfast determination hidden behind the numbers and awards. It's a story of long hours spent honing her talent, early morning workouts, and late-night sessions. It's a tale of unwavering self-belief, coaching advice, and familial support.

Chapter 1: A Small-Town Beginning

Caitlin's Early Years in Iowa

Caitlin Clark grew up in West Des Moines after being born in Des Moines, Iowa, on January 22, 2002. When she was five years old, she was first introduced to basketball and joined boys' leisure teams since there were no appropriate girls' leagues.

In addition to basketball, Clark experimented with softball, volleyball, soccer, tennis and golf as a kid before settling on basketball as her main activity.

By the time Clark reached thirteen, she was participating in girls' leagues many years ahead of her age group, demonstrating extraordinary skill and determination. She started playing basketball with the All Iowa Attack, a prestigious AAU programme based in Ames, Iowa, in the sixth grade.

Clark thrived in the Attack programme under coach Dickson Jensen's tutelage, as did her friend and eventual WNBA star Ashley Joens.

Inspired by Minnesota Lynx star Maya Moore, a WNBA player, Clark went above and beyond to see her dad play, often traveling great distances to see them play. She also looked up to All Iowa Attack alum Harrison Barnes, and once Barnes joined the Tar Heels, she became an avid supporter of the team.

Caitlin Clark's love of basketball and her unwavering drive for perfection throughout her formative years set the stage for her incredible path in the game.

Caitlin Clark's trip started in the charming settings of a little town in Iowa, deep in the heart of the country's stunning landscapes. Caitlin's early years were filled with the coziness and ease of country living, having been raised in a close-knit neighborhood where everyone knew one another by name and the restaurant served as the center of social life.

Caitlin was raised in a home that reflected the enduring traditions of Midwestern values, emphasizing persistence, hard work, and honesty from a young age. She grew up surrounded by acres and acres of cornfields that stretched forever, and she got her passion and commitment from her parents, who were also strong members of the community.

These beautiful surroundings were the beginning of Caitlin's love affair with basketball. She fell in love with the rhythm of the game as soon as she could hold a ball in her little hands.

She loved the sound of the audience roaring, the squeak of shoes on hardwood floors and the thump of the ball on the backboard.

Caitlin's love for high school basketball was sparked by seeing elite players light up the floor in the glow of the gymnasium lights, in a community where Friday evenings were set aside for the sport. She was motivated by their tenacity and skill and hoped to emulate them in the future by making her own contributions to the game.

Caitlin's passion had no limits, even with the few resources and possibilities available to athletes in a tiny town. She took advantage of every opportunity to hone her talents, whether it was late-night game tape study sessions or hoops in the driveway till dusk, all with the unshakable support of her family and coaches.

Caitlin's aspirations became brighter as the sun sank on yet another day in rural Iowa, strengthening her resolve to overcome the challenges and forge her own route to success. She had no idea that her modest upbringing would lay the groundwork for a path that would propel her to the top of the basketball world and inspire innumerable others in the process.

Chapter 2: Hoops and Dreams

Caitlin's Introduction to Basketball

It seemed like destiny had stepped in and lit a flame that would fire Caitlin Clark's love for basketball years before she ever lay eyes on one.

Caitlin's introduction to basketball was rather fortunate, given her upbringing in the Midwest of Iowa, where daily routines were as predictable as the endless expanses of cornfields.

When Caitlin was five years old, she happened to find a worn-out basketball hidden in the corner of her family's garage on a clear autumn day. Captivated by its recognisable but enigmatic form, she extended her arm to take hold of it in her little hands, feeling an unexplainable bond emerge inside her.

Caitlin felt a surge of excitement shooting through her veins with every shot she took, a sudden sensation of thrill with each dribble of the ball on the broken pavement of her driveway.

She was soon enthralled with the sport, spending many hours improving her shot and dribble, and dreaming of the day she would grace the floor with her presence. Her father's soft encouragement and steadfast support guided her throughout this process.

Caitlin's enthusiasm for basketball only grew as the years and the seasons changed, turning it from a light hobby into a full-fledged obsession.

Driven by an unwavering drive to succeed, she threw her heart and soul into the game, practicing layups in the dimly lit gymnasiums of her little town and shooting baskets beneath the streetlights.

Caitlin's aspirations became more lofty as time went on, driven by the limitless opportunities that awaited her. She had no idea that her modest upbringing would lay the groundwork for a journey that would propel her to the pinnacles of the basketball world and inspire innumerable others in the process. So Caitlin Clark set off on a voyage that would alter her life forever, with a ball in hand and a heart full of hopes.

Chapter 3: Rising Through the Ranks

Caitlin's High School Career

Under the direction of head coach Kristin Meyer, Clark played varsity basketball for four years at Dowling Catholic High School in West Des Moines.

Her first season, in which she averaged 15.3 points, 4.7 assists, and 2.3 steals per game, demonstrated her emerging ability. Her outstanding performance earned her an honorable mention in The Des Moines Register's All-Iowa list and distinction as a member of the Iowa Newspaper Association's Class 5A All-State third team.

In the first round of the state tournament, Dowling was defeated by eventual winners, Valley High School, despite a heroic effort.

The next season, Clark's influence became even more apparent. With a remarkable average of 27.1 points, 6.5 rebounds, 4 assists, and 2.3 steals per game, she was awarded Central Iowa Metro League Player of the Year by The Des Moines Register and earned first-team Class 5A All-State honors by the Iowa Print Sports Writers Association.

She also was a key component in Dowling's run to the state quarterfinals and helped All Iowa Attack win the Nike Elite Youth Basketball League title.

During her junior year, Clark made basketball history at Iowa with an incredible show of ability. With 13 three-pointers, she broke a state record and recorded the second-highest single-game point total with her game-high 60 points.

She proceeded to dominate, setting a single-game scoring record of 42 points in the Class 5A state tournament.

She averaged 32.6 points per game throughout the season, which led the state in scoring. She was named the Iowa Gatorade Player of the

Year and was selected to the first team of the Class 5A All-State team.

Clark continued to be excellent in her senior year, scoring 33.4 points a night to help her team to a 19–4 record. Her incredible career resulted with several awards, including Iowa Gatorade Player of the Year, Des Moines Register All-Iowa Athlete of the Year, and Iowa Miss Basketball, despite a devastating defeat in the regional final.

Selections to participate in two prominent high school all-star games—the Jordan Brand Classic and the McDonald's All-American Game—which were sadly postponed due to the COVID-19 epidemic served as further evidence of her accomplishments.

Caitlin's High School Career

In addition to hoops, Clark demonstrated her flexibility as an athlete by succeeding in her first two years as a starter on Dowling's varsity soccer team. In only her first season, she scored 23 goals and was named to The Des Moines Register's Class 3A All-Iowa squad.

Even before Caitlin Clark started high school, NCAA Division I programmes were taking notice of her skills on the basketball floor. An early letter of interest from Missouri State, which she received prior to her seventh-grade year, started her recruiting process.

Her abilities and performance carried her to the top of the rankings as her time at Dowling

Catholic High School grew. She was regarded as the top player in the 2020 high school class by ESPN by the time she entered her second year.

Caitlin had established herself as a five-star prospect by the time her high school career came to an end, and ESPN ranked her as the fourth-best player in her graduating class. She made a crucial choice on November 12, 2019, when she declared her intention to play collegiate basketball for Iowa.

Caitlin was lured to Iowa by head coach Lisa Bluder's up-tempo offense and her ability to produce point guards, even though she had offers from Iowa State and Notre Dame.

Caitlin's choice was also impacted by the chance to have an instant effect on the group.

As the current Big Ten Player of the Year, Kathleen Doyle, left, Caitlin saw an opportunity to assume a significant role early in her collegiate career.

Her interest in the University of Iowa Hawkeyes was solidified by the combination of coaching compatibility, playing style, and the opportunity to help a team achieve success.

Chapter 4: The Decision

Iowa Hawkeyes outstanding player Caitlin Clark is on the verge of shattering the all-time scoring record and establishing her own chapter in college basketball history.

When Clark was a high school student at Dowling Catholic High School, she was courted by several prestigious programmes, but in the end, she chose to wear the black and gold of the Hawkeyes.

In light of her choice, Clark stressed the value of performing for fervent audiences and flourishing in the electrifying environment of crowded gyms. "If anybody watched me in high school, they know that I live in a packed gym," she said. "To be honest, the women's basketball team at Iowa has excellent support, which is one of the reasons I came here. I just thrive in chaotic gatherings."

Even though many programmes that had won national championships were fighting for her skill, Clark was lured to Iowa because of the school's distinct culture and attitude. "I refused to follow in everyone else's footsteps.

That is a small portion of my tale, and it is one of the reasons I traveled to Iowa. It really fits with who I am," the woman said.

Her decision was greatly influenced by Clark's decision to remain near her home. "I could have gone pretty much anywhere after high school. She said, "I love my team, I love the

University of Iowa, and I love the people." "I can see my family all the time because I live so close to home." I really think that this is the best location for me, to be honest. Although I had a wonderful first year, I believe that our second year will be much better.

Caitlin Clark is driven by her team's support, her fans' devotion, and her love for her home state to keep making her imprint on the court with unflinching confidence and a strong feeling of belonging.

Choosing the Path to College Basketball

Caitlin Clark's choice to play collegiate basketball was a turning point in her life that was driven by a strong sense of purpose, serious thought, and passionate contemplation.

Caitlin's path to this point had taken years; it was the result of many hours on the court, sacrifices, and ambitions fostered.

As the NCAA Division I offers started rolling in, Caitlin was forced to make a decision that would determine the course of her career. Every institution offered something different and alluring, with the promise of a combination of sports growth, intellectual brilliance, and friendship. However, among all the choices, one stuck out as being particularly noteworthy: the University of Iowa.

Caitlin's choice to attend Iowa was motivated by more than just practicality or closeness; rather, it was a deeply held belief based on a philosophy of coaching that matched her ideals and her own goals.

Caitlin was drawn to Iowa because of the Hawkeyes' fast-paced brand of basketball and head coach Lisa Bluder's well-known leadership. She regarded Iowa as the ideal backdrop for her college basketball career.

Furthermore, Caitlin saw Iowa as a place where she could have a direct effect and advance quickly—a programme with a long history of quality, and an opportunity to assume a leadership position right away. Following Big Ten Player of the Year Kathleen Doyle's retirement, Caitlin regarded herself as the heir apparent, ready to continue the tradition of Hawkeye excellence.

But beyond the numbers and honors was a deeper reality: Caitlin made her choice out of a genuine passion for the game and a desire to challenge herself, not because she was promised fame or recognition.

It was an action motivated by ambition, passion, and the conviction that the voyage would be just as fulfilling as the final destination.

Caitlin Clark decided to wear the black and gold of the Iowa Hawkeyes, starting a new chapter in her basketball career that would be full of obstacles, victories, and the unyielding quest of excellence.

This choice was made with a strong sense of purpose blazing brightly inside her.

Chapter 5: The Freshman Phenom

Clark started as the University of Iowa's starting point guard in her first year. On November 25, 2020, she made her college debut, displaying her skills in a convincing 96-81 win against Northern Iowa with 27 points, 8 rebounds, and 4 assists.

A week later, on December 2, in an exciting 103–97 victory against Drake, Clark recorded her maiden double-double with an outstanding 30 points and 13 assists.

On December 22, Clark made history in Iowa's record books with the program's first triple-double since 2015. It was an unforgettable performance.

She struggled with her shooting, but she still managed to score 13 points, grab 13 rebounds, and dish out 10 assists in a convincing 92–65 win against Western Illinois.

On January 6, 2021, Clark continued to amaze on the court. He had 37 points, 11 rebounds, and four assists in a commanding 92–79 victory against Minnesota.

In an 88-81 win against Nebraska on February 11, she turned in one of her best performances of the year, setting a new single-game scoring record at Pinnacle Bank Arena, home of

Nebraska, with an incredible 39 points, 10 rebounds, and seven assists.

Clark received the proper recognition for his outstanding performances as the regular season came to an end. She was selected to the first team All-Big Ten and received unanimous recognition as the Big Ten Freshman of the Year.

Setting a conference record and topping the Big Ten with five Player of the Week trophies, Clark's incredible season was further emphasized by her amazing total of 13 Big Ten Freshman of the Week awards.

Caitlin's Arrival at the University of Iowa

Clark was a key player in Iowa's outstanding Big Ten tournament performance, which helped them place second. She was named to the all-tournament team for her outstanding play, and she also established a new record with the most assists ever recorded in the history of the competition—37.

Clark put on an incredible performance in the second round of the NCAA tournament, scoring 35 points, grabbing seven rebounds, and dishing out six assists as her team defeated Kentucky 86–72.

She notably shattered the program's single-game records for points and three-pointers, making a total of six of them throughout the competition.

Iowa's odyssey came to an end in the Sweet 16 when they faced first-seeded UConn, a difficult opponent despite the team's heroic efforts. Clark however kept up his impressive play, scoring 21 points in the 92–72 defeat.

Her exceptional play throughout the season won her two major honors: the United States Basketball Writers Association (USBWA) designated her a first-team All-American, and the Associated Press (AP) placed her on the roster of the second team All-American.

Clark also guaranteed her spot on the Coaches' All-America team of the Women's Basketball Coaches Association (WBCA).

As a rookie, Clark made history by winning the coveted Dawn Staley Award, which is given to the top Division I guard. She was the first freshman to get this award.

To further underscore her outstanding first season, Clark and Paige Bueckers of UConn were jointly named Division I Freshman of the Year recipients of the Tamika Catchings honor (given by the USBWA) and the WBCA Freshman of the Year honor.

With remarkable game averages of 26.6 points, 7.1 assists, and 5.9 rebounds, Clark's statistical influence was evident.

In addition to being second in assists and three-pointers made per game, she topped the NCAA Division I in scoring. Her point, assist, field goal, and three-pointer totals also led the Division I charts. With the fourth-highest scoring average in the school's history, Clark made a lasting impression on Iowa basketball history by breaking records for points and assists as a freshman.

- **Sophomore Season**

Caitlin Clark had a spectacular comeback for her sophomore season on November 9, 2021, with 26 points, eight rebounds, and six assists in a convincing 93–50 win against New Hampshire. In a decisive 93–56 victory against Evansville, two months later on January 2, 2022, she once again demonstrated her scoring ability with 44 points and eight assists.

On January 2, 2022, Clark made history at Carver-Hawkeye Arena when she broke the record for women's single-game scoring and became the first Big Ten player to achieve 1,000 points in her career, surpassing Ohio State's Kelsey Mitchell.

In keeping with her incredible season, Clark recorded her fourth triple-double of the year on January 16, 2022, going above and above with 31 points, 10 rebounds, and 10 assists in a spirited 93–83 victory against Nebraska.

Four days later, she created history once again by scoring at least thirty points in three straight triple-doubles, a feat never before seen in Division I men's or women's basketball. She also accomplished a notable first for women's players in Big Ten history by being the first.

Award after award came in for Clark's outstanding play. She dominated with 18 assists on January 25, breaking conference and programme single-game records.

She also added 20 points and 7 rebounds in a commanding 107–79 win against Penn State.

Clark had fierce competition, but his genius never wavered. She demonstrated her scoring ability once again on January 31, with 43 points, seven assists, and four rebounds in a valiant 92-88 defeat to Ohio State.

Notwithstanding the failures, on February 6, 2022, Clark turned in a game-changing effort that would go down in history. She scored an incredible 46 points, including 25 in the fourth quarter, and dished out 10 assists in a dramatic 98-90 defeat to Michigan. Her outstanding performance broke the previous women's single-game scoring record at Michigan's home venue, Crisler Centre.

Clark's extraordinary efforts were recognised when she was unanimously selected Big Ten Player of the Year and was nominated to the first team of the Big Ten by the media and coaches.

This incredible season was capped off with several record-breaking accomplishments and memorable memories.

Caitlin Clark put on a spectacular performance in the Big Ten tournament quarterfinals on March 5, 2022, scoring 41 points and grabbing nine rebounds to help her team defeat Nebraska 83–66. Along with guaranteeing Iowa's spot in the tournament championship game, Clark's outstanding performance earned him the honor of being voted the Most Outstanding Player (MOP) of the event.

Tenth-seeded Creighton beat Iowa in the second round of the NCAA tournament, despite her outstanding individual performance.

Clark was limited to a season-low 15 points and 11 assists in this game. Her team lost by a slim margin of 64–62 as a consequence of her poor shooting performance (4 of 19).

Nevertheless, Clark's outstanding season-long play was acknowledged despite the loss. She was recognized by the U.S. Basketball Writers Association (USBWA) and the Associated Press (AP) as a unanimous first-team All-American. She was also chosen for the Coaches' All-America Team of the Women's Basketball Coaches Association (WBCA).

In addition, Clark's outstanding sophomore year was capped off with a number of noteworthy honors, such as being the first person to win the Dawn Staley Award twice in a row and taking home the Nancy Lieberman Award, which is given to the best Division I point guard.

She became the first women's athlete to top Division I in both points and assists per game in a single season with her incredible 27 points, eight rebounds, and eight assists per game average. Her statistical accomplishments were equally astounding. She also set Division I records for total points, free throws, and numerous triple-doubles, enhancing her reputation as one of the most explosive players in the game.

- **Junior Season**

As she entered her junior year, Caitlin Clark was well-known, having been named unanimously to the AP preseason All-America team and having won the Big Ten preseason player of the year award from the league's coaches and media.

Though Clark had an outstanding game, finishing with 27 points, 10 rebounds, and 7 assists, she suffered an ankle injury with just a few seconds left on November 18, 2022, against Kansas State.

Despite her injury, Clark showed her tenacity by playing in Iowa's next game against

Belmont on November 20. In a thrilling 73–62 win, Clark scored 33 points in an incredible display of play. In a valiant effort to lose 94–81 against NC State, she scored a season-high 45 points on December 1, little over a week later.

On December 4, Clark recorded her ninth career triple-double in a dominant 102–71 win against Wisconsin. She did it by dishing out 10 rebounds, 10 assists, and 22 points. She also beat Samantha Logic to become the career triple-double leader in the Big Ten.

As she continued her incredible season, Clark on December 21 tied Delaware's Elena Delle Donne for the fastest Division I women's player to reach 2,000 career points since the 1999–2000 campaign. Clark accomplished this feat in her 75th game, a 92–54 victory over Dartmouth.

The enthusiasm only grew when Clark's incredible performance against AP No. 2 Ohio State on January 23, 2023, with an outstanding 28 points, 15 assists, and 10 rebounds in a noteworthy 83–72 triumph over the undefeated squad.

After this incredible performance, Clark had another one on February 2, going into a comfortable 96-82 win against Maryland with 42 points, eight assists, and seven rebounds.

With the regular season coming to an end, Clark cemented her place among the best players in college hoops by winning the Big Ten Player of the Year award in a unanimous vote for the second year running. She was further recognized for her domination and influence on the game when the coaches and media in the league nominated her to the first team of the Big Ten.

Showing off her skills on the court and winning the Most Outstanding Player (MOP) award, Clark led Iowa to its second straight Big Ten tournament title. She put on an outstanding effort in the championship game against Ohio State, scoring 30 points, dishing out 17 assists, and grabbing 10 rebounds in a decisive 105–72 win.

This incredible performance was the first triple-double in the tournament final, and it catapulted Clark to the second-best career triple-double position in Division I women's basketball history, behind only Oregon's Sabrina Ionescu.

Clark put on another incredible display in the NCAA tournament's Elite Eight, scoring 41 points, dishing out 12 assists, and grabbing 10 rebounds in a decisive 97-83 victory against Louisville.

She once again made history with her incredible performance, becoming the first player in men's or women's tournament history to achieve a triple-double of 30 or 40 points.

Clark accomplished a historic feat in this game by becoming the first Division I player to record at least 900 points and 300 assists in a single season.

Acknowledging her outstanding contributions, Iowa won its first Final Four participation since 1993, and she was awarded the Seattle 4 Regional MOP.

Clark displayed her skills once again in the Final Four semifinal game, with 41 points, eight assists, and six rebounds in an exciting 77-73 shock win over the unbeaten South Carolina team.

Her accomplishment broke the women's tournament semifinals single-game scoring record and became the first player in tournament history to have back-to-back 40-point games.

To further highlight her supremacy on the court, Clark broke Megan Gustafson's single-season scoring records for the Big Ten and the program. Iowa's victory put the program on the path to its first-ever women's basketball championship game.

Clark put in a heroic effort, but Iowa lost 102–85 to LSU in the national championship game. However, Clark's remarkable shooting ability was on display as she sank eight three-pointers, tying the record for the most three-pointers made by a player in a championship game—male or female.

As the final game was coming to a close, LSU standout Angel Reese made disparaging gestures against Clark. This event brought attention to the complexity of the world of elite athletics by sparking a discussion on gender, racism, and sportsmanship.

On the biggest platform in college basketball, Clark's performance throughout the tournament was nothing short of historic as she broke scoring records and displayed her unmatched skill set.

Throughout her NCAA basketball career, Clark won every major national player of the year award, demonstrating her extraordinary achievement.

Her outstanding list of accolades included the Wade Trophy, the Naismith College Player of the Year, the Honda Sports Award, the John R. Wooden Award, the AP Player of the Year, and the USBWA National Player of the Year. She was notable for being the first-ever unanimous national player of the year in Big Ten annals.

She won important honors twice for her domination on the court, including the Dawn

Staley Award and the Nancy Lieberman Award, which she received three times in a row. She also received unanimous first-team All-American acclaim for the second season in a row from the USBWA, the AP, and the WBCA Coaches' All-America Team.

Clark's outstanding play during her junior year demonstrated her flexibility as she averaged a game-high 27.8 points, 8.6 assists, and 7.1 rebounds.

She was second in scoring and first in assists in Division I. She established many noteworthy records, including single-season highs in the Big Ten for points, assists, three-pointers, and free throws.

She also equaled the conference record for triple-doubles with five, confirming her reputation as an outstanding player.

Her statistical accomplishments, which ranked her fourth in points and assists and third in three-pointers made in a single season, elevated her to the top in Division I history.

Her exceptional achievements were properly acknowledged with prestigious honors including the Honda Cup, the Best Female College Athlete ESPY Award, and the James E. Sullivan Award, which is given out yearly by the AAU to the best college or Olympic athlete in the country.

She also won the Big Ten Female Athlete of the Year award, solidifying her reputation as one of the most accomplished players in college athletics.

- ## Senior Season

Caitlin Clark made a big impression in her last season, winning unanimous AP preseason All-American and preseason Big Ten Player of the Year. She demonstrated her abilities at the Crossover at Kinnick, a preseason exhibition game at Kinnick Stadium versus DePaul, on October 15, 2023.

Clark put on a spectacular talent show as she recorded a triple-double with 34 points, 11 rebounds, and 10 assists, helping her side to a commanding 94–72 win. A record-breaking 55,646 people watched the game, which established a new attendance record for women's basketball.

Clark's influence extended beyond the court throughout the season, particularly impacting ticket sales, which led to the creation of the "Caitlin Clark effect." Iowa had a spike in home game attendance, selling out every game for the first time ever.

A further indication of Clark's star power is the increase in attendance that other teams saw while hosting the Hawkeyes.

On November 9, in Iowa's second regular-season game against AP No. 8 Virginia Tech, Clark had a spectacular game, with 44 points, eight rebounds, and six assists to help Iowa defeat the team 80–76.

Three days later, she had her 12th career triple-double with 24 points, 11 assists, and 10 rebounds against Northern Iowa in a commanding 94–53 victory. With this achievement, she also surpassed Gustafson to become Iowa's all-time top scorer.

In addition, Clark entered exclusive company when he and Ionescu became the first players in Division I history to post a triple-double in four separate seasons.

On November 19, Clark created history once again with her incredible performance. She finished with 35 points, 10 assists, 6 rebounds, and 7 steals in a decisive 113-90 win over Drake. She cemented her place as one of the best players in the game by surpassing Kelsey Plum of Washington for the most

30-point games in women's Division I history with her accomplishment.

On December 6, 2023, Caitlin Clark became the 15th Division I player to reach 3,000 career points in basketball. This was a huge accomplishment for her career. She did it in spectacular fashion, dishing up nine rebounds, five assists, and 35 points in a crucial 67-58 win against Iowa State.

Ten days later, Clark once again demonstrated her scoring ability, scoring 38 points and making nine three-pointers in an outstanding 104-75 victory against Cleveland State.

Quickly after, Clark received recognition for her exceptional athletic accomplishments when, on December 19, she and Angel Reese shared the coveted Sporting News Athlete of the Year title.

She also received recognition for her outstanding performance on the basketball court as the runner-up for the AP Female Athlete of the Year award, behind gymnast Simone Biles.

On December 21, Clark had an incredible performance that left spectators and commentators in awe. She recorded a triple-double with 35 points, 17 rebounds, and 10 assists in a convincing 98-69 win against Loyola Chicago.

She finished the game on December 30 with 35 points and 10 assists, overtaking Ohio State's Samantha Prahalis to become the Big Ten's all-time assist leader.

That game was against Minnesota. In addition, Clark broke Samantha Logic's program record in the same category during this game, cemented her legacy as an Iowa basketball legend.

Clark's success in the new year began on January 2, 2024, when she showed off her clutch ability by scoring 40 points and making the game-winning three-pointer with seconds remaining in a dramatic 76-73 victory against Michigan State.

Three days later, she showed off her flexibility once again, leading Rutgers to a decisive 103-69 victory with 29 points, 10 rebounds, and 10 assists.

Accolades for her outstanding work kept coming in; on January 8, Clark was selected Big Ten Player of the Week for the 24th time in her career, shattering Gustafson's previous conference record.

Despite the recognition, she persisted in her impressive streak, recording her second straight triple-double on January 11 in a dominating 96–71 win against Purdue with 26 points, 10 rebounds, and 10 assists.

But even in the middle of her incredible success, Clark also encountered misfortune on January 21 when, after a standout game against AP No. 18 Ohio State, she was tripped and fell by a supporter as the other team's fans flooded the court in celebration.

Thankfully, Clark survived the early worries about her health and showed her tenacity on and off the court.

Caitlin Clark put on a spectacular display on January 31, 2024, scoring 35 points and dishing out 10 assists in a commanding 110–74 win against Northwestern.

With her incredible performance, she not only helped her team win big but also achieved a historic first by breaking the Big Ten scoring record.

Held by Ohio State's Kelsey Mitchell before, Clark's accomplishment cemented her reputation as one of the conference's most prolific scorers ever.

Chapter 6: Mastering the Game

Basketball skill is an art form that requires a careful balancing act between natural ability and unwavering effort. Every dribble, pass, and shot Caitlin Clark makes on the floor demonstrates this proficiency.

Caitlin has developed her play style to a point where it is all her own, thanks to a mix of innate talent and many hours of effort.

The secret to Caitlin's success is her unmatched ability to score goals. She has a lethal precise shooting range and an amazing aptitude for finding the hoop. Her offensive arsenal intimidates opposition defenses. Caitlin's scoring ability is incredible, whether she's launching three-pointers from beyond the arc or cutting through the defense with blazing drives to the basket.

However, Caitlin's skill goes much beyond just recording points. She is a real floor general with a basketball IQ that defies her age, directing the attack with grace and accuracy.

She has an intuitive ability to read the game and make split-second judgments that put her team one step ahead of the opposition. Her eyes are continuously scanning the court, and her mind is always thinking several movements ahead.

However, Caitlin's constant dedication to growth and her unrelenting work ethic may be what really set her apart. Despite her dominance on the court, she never sits back and keeps pushing herself to improve her abilities and achieve new heights.

Caitlin's commitment to her art is admirable, whether it's working out additional hours to hone her shot or watching game tape to analyze her opponent's defenses.

Caitlin's Skills and Style on the Court

Caitlin enters the court on game day with a calm assurance, knowing that she has worked hard to achieve. She oozes confidence with every dribble, certain that she has the abilities and intelligence to conquer any obstacle in her path. Caitlin's status as one of basketball's biggest stars only becomes stronger every day as she continues to hone the sport.

The audience gasps in anticipation as Caitlin Clark enters the court because of her incredible passing ability as well as her exceptional long-range shooting.

Though her long 3-pointers are well-deserved recognition, her brilliant passes, whether made in transition or behind the back, are what really make her stand out.

Clark's scoring prowess and NBA-caliber shooting range have won him recognition as an All-America guard. Her outstanding passing abilities, however, are just as crucial to Iowa's success on the court.

Defenses that oppose her often concentrate their efforts on keeping Clark and her pick-and-roll partner, Monika Czinano, in check. However, Clark's ability to find open teammates in the middle of dense defensive coverage has continuously advanced the Hawkeyes' offensive line.

Throughout Iowa's run to the Sweet 16, her skill at threading the needle and seeing passing lanes when none seem to exist has confused opponents.

Clark's versatile game, which is shown by her smart passing and scoring ability, is crucial to the second-seeded Hawkeyes' chances of winning on the national stage as they get ready to play No. 6 Colorado.

Caitlin Clark places a high value on comfort, style, and performance in her footwear to complement her explosive play on the basketball court. Caitlin, who is well-known for her quickness and agility, needs shoes that can keep up with her level of intensity while providing the support she needs.

Caitlin's preferred option? Her go-to clothing brand for effortlessly balancing style and performance is the Nike Kyrie collection.

Caitlin can perform fast moves with ease because of the Nike Kyrie sneakers' responsive design and lightweight construction, which improves her agility and speed on the court.

In particular, Caitlin often chooses the Nike Kyrie 7 trainers, which are well-known for their superb grip, agile cushioning, and snug fit. These characteristics help her perform better while also making sure she feels safe and at ease over long gaming sessions.

For athletes like Caitlin who are looking for a combination of elegance and practicality, the Nike Kyrie 7s are a top option because of its sophisticated design and cutting-edge technology.

Caitlin knows she can improve her game by wearing her Nike Kyrie 7s because of their dependability and effectiveness, whether she's driving to the basket or running down the court.

The shoes' lightweight and breathable construction allows for maximum ventilation, which keeps Caitlin's feet cool and lowers the possibility of pain or injury during extended play.

Caitlin can wear stability while she maneuvers the demands of the game with grace and accuracy thanks to the Nike Kyrie 7s' tight lacing system, which offers a snug and supportive fit.

Chapter 7: Overcoming Obstacles

Caitlin Clark had a number of difficulties and trials throughout her career as a basketball player; each one tested her fortitude and tenacity.

Caitlin encountered obstacles along the road, but her persistent attitude and unrelenting work ethic kept her moving ahead and helped her transform hardships into chances for personal growth.

The lack of girls' basketball leagues in Caitlin's early years was one of the biggest obstacles she had to overcome. She was unfazed by this restriction and chose to participate in guys' leisure leagues rather than follow social conventions.

Her determination was strengthened by this experience, and she also improved her abilities as a result of learning how to play in a highly competitive setting.

Caitlin faced additional challenges when she made the switch to girls' leagues, including more intense competition and mounting performance expectations. She didn't let the challenges stop her; instead, she used them as fuel for her fire, pushing herself to reach new heights throughout practice and competition.

Caitlin had to deal with difficulties off the court as well as personal ones, such as setbacks and injuries. These experiences put her tenacity and mental toughness to the test, requiring her to face hardship head-on and come out stronger on the other side.

Caitlin learned important lessons about tenacity, patience, and the strength of resilience by using setbacks as chances for reflection and personal development rather than letting them define her.

Caitlin never faltered in her steadfast conviction in herself and her ability throughout it all.

She faced every challenge head-on, never letting anything get in the way of her goals, with the help of her family, coaches, and teammates. And by doing this, Caitlin not only became a strong athlete but also a bright example of perseverance, encouraging people to face their own obstacles head-on and follow their hobbies with unflinching fervor.

Caitlin's Challenges and Resilience

Caitlin Clark is getting closer to breaking the all-time NCAA women's basketball scoring record by 66 points, and she is about to make history.

Barring any unexpected setbacks, she is on course to break records in the next few weeks, maintaining an astounding average of 32.4 points per game.

Her tremendous skill has not only brought attention to women's college basketball but has also received worldwide recognition, as seen by her recent performances in terms of viewing, which have surpassed those of NBA games.

Even yet, Clark has been involved in controversy, receiving unfair criticism from former WNBA star Sheryl Swoopes despite her unquestionable accomplishments.

Swoopes' derogatory remarks aimed to downplay Clark's achievements by disseminating false information about her professional background and raising questions about her reliability as a seasoned player.

This critique, which has overtones of racism, highlights a greater problem of prejudice in the sports world.

Similar to the difficulties faced by well-known NBA players like Nikola Jokic and Luka Doncic, Clark has experienced suspicion and animosity as a white athlete succeeding in a traditionally black player-dominated sport.

As Clark makes the move to the WNBA, experts like Jason Whitlock and Steve Kim predict that she may run against bigotry and opposition from other LGBTQ players.

Notwithstanding these obstacles, Clark's path sheds light on the complex interactions between gender, racism, and sportsmanship in the modern sporting world.

Her tenacity and commitment serve as evidence of her unshakable commitment to the sport she loves, as she pushes limits and resets records.

Chapter 8: A Leader Emerges

Not only did Caitlin Clarke carry her own goals and desires when she stepped onto the court, but she also carried the dreams and hopes of her teammates.

Leading in athletics involves more than simply calling plays and scoring points; it also entails motivating others to reach their greatest potential and creating a feeling of togetherness and purpose that goes beyond individual accomplishments.

Caitlin accepted her position as a leader with resolute conviction and poise the moment she put on her team's shirt.

She set an example for her teammates by being resilient, determined, and unselfish, whether it was during stressful times on the court or when she was giving words of support in the locker room.

However, leadership is more than simply what occurs on game day; it also involves the many hours of sacrifice and commitment that go into the background.

Caitlin set an example for her colleagues by being the first to come to practice and the last to depart, showing them the value of dedication and hard effort in the quest of greatness.

However, genuine leadership involves more than simply pressuring people to achieve; it also entails helping them up when they fall and providing support and direction when they face difficulties.

Caitlin was aware of this without being asked, supporting her colleagues in times of uncertainty and doubt by reassuring them of their combined fortitude and resilience.

Outside of the game, Caitlin demonstrated leadership by using her position to support issues that were important to her.

She was an inspiration to others because she lived up to the ideals of empathy and compassion, whether it was by standing up against injustice or giving to those in need.

Ultimately, Caitlin Clarke's leadership impact extends beyond the basketball floor. She served as a living example of the transforming power of leadership for all of us, demonstrating that genuine greatness isn't determined by points scored or games won but rather by the lives touched and hearts inspired along the journey.

Caitlin's Role as Team Captain

Caitlin Clark represented the US in a number of FIBA events, showcasing her skills on the global scale.

During the FIBA Under-16 Women's Americas Championship in Buenos Aires, Argentina in 2017, she made a significant contribution as a substitute player. Clark contributed significantly to her team's perfect 5–0 record and gold medal win, averaging 8.8 points per game.

Clark maintained her success on the international front two years later in Bangkok, Thailand, in the 2019 FIBA Under-19 Women's Basketball World Cup.

Even though she was a young player, she showed her flexibility by scoring 5.3 points per game, which helped her team win another gold medal with a perfect 7-0 record.

Clark wore the USA jersey at Debrecen, Hungary, in 2021 during the FIBA Under-19

Women's Basketball World Cup. She won the gold medal for her squad and demonstrated her extraordinary abilities by averaging a remarkable 14.3 points, 5.6 assists, and 5.3 rebounds per game.

Thanks to her outstanding play, Clark was named the Most Valuable Player and earned a berth on the All-Tournament Team.

Caitlin Clark plays a dynamic style of basketball that is defined by her ability to cut quickly, set screens well, distribute the ball precisely to teammates, and sink long-range three-point goals, including buzzer-beaters.

She moves the ball relentlessly on the court, making it difficult for opponents to stop her as she looks to generate scoring chances for both herself and her team.

Clark stressed her dedication to never stopping moving in an interview with LaChina Robinson, Zora Stephenson, and Isis Young. She said, "I never want to stop moving... It's not that I was always good at moving, and I don't believe it was always my intention, but I feel like I have no choice but to keep going because everyone is after me and I have to make it difficult for them."

There is no denying Caitlin Clark's influence on the court. Her role as the Hawkeyes' top player in college basketball has been solidified as she led the team to an incredible 18-1 overall record, including a perfect 7-0 record in Big Ten play.

Notably, in November Clark became the all-time leader in scoring at Iowa, surpassing

Megan Gustafson. She also made history by being the first player in Division I history to amass more than 3,000 points, 900 assists, and 800 rebounds in a career.

She also became one of only a few select NCAA women's basketball players to score more than 3,000 points, and she most recently overtook Brittney Griner to take fourth position on the all-time scoring list.

With their recent winning streak behind them, Caitlin Clark and her Iowa teammates are riding high as they get ready to play in the Schottenstein Centre in Columbus, Ohio.

But the season got off with its own set of difficulties, especially when important players like McKenna Warnock and veteran Monika Czinano left. Given this, Clark accepted his newly discovered leadership position within the squad.

"I've had to step up and become more vocal, especially with the younger players," said Clark. "They turn to me for direction and encouragement, particularly when things become tight on the court.

It's about giving them confidence, telling them that their efforts count, and motivating them to keep moving ahead."

Three years of cohesiveness and camaraderie had preceded this season for Iowa's starting team. But Clark understands that the team's performance depends on the growth and self-assurance of players who haven't yet faced stressful circumstances.

Clark keeps becoming better on her own as a leader as she takes on more responsibilities. With 3,527 points, Kelsey Plum presently holds the NCAA all-time scoring record, which she is attempting to break.

But for Clark, the primary objective is still to win every game with her squad.

Chapter 9: Shining Bright

In the national championship game versus LSU, Caitlin Clark suffered a heartbreaking 102-85 loss. Nevertheless, despite the sadness, one thing is still quite evident: her impact goes beyond the outcome.

Clark, a native of Des Moines, has gained notoriety over the last three weeks because of her outstanding performance.

Her amazing long-range shoots and brilliant transition passes have enthralled spectators and brought her international acclaim.

Basketball greats like Magic Johnson and Steph Curry have been all over Clark's praise.

Famous for her incredible passing ability, she has been compared to basketball great "Pistol" Pete Maravich, which has earned her the nickname "Ponytail Pete."

Clark's charm has only grown as a result of her on-court bluster and her readiness to interact with supporters both on and off the court.

In anticipation of seeing Clark's dynamic gameplay, almost 6 million people tuned in to see the semifinal matchup between South Carolina and Clark. As expected, she put on a spectacular display, giving up eight assists and scoring an astounding 41 points.

Clark broke tournament records along the way, breaking the marks for most 3-pointers made and most points scored in a single tournament. But she has always wanted to have a significant influence; she has never been concerned with individual recognition.

After losing the title, Clark thought back on her journey and said that she wanted her legacy to go well beyond the basketball court. She expressed her desire to motivate young, aspiring athletes, particularly those from her own Iowa, while crying.

She said it so beautifully: "I want my influence on Iowans and young children to be my legacy. Once, I was that little girl. To experience moments like this, all you need to do is dream."

Caitlin Clark dazzles the basketball floor with her brilliant prowess in every game, leaving onlookers in awe of her extraordinary skills.

She has continuously turned up performances that not only highlight her talent but also shatter records over her career.

From her earliest basketball days to her time as a student at the University of Iowa, Caitlin has made a lasting impression with her ability to score baskets, create plays, and unwavering perseverance.

She has created new standards and raised the bar for perfection with each dribble, pass, and shot that she has made, leaving her stamp on the annals of basketball history.

Caitlin had incredible scoring adventures throughout her high school years. Scouts and supporters alike took notice of her as she consistently lit up the scoreboard with her accurate shooting and inventive offensive play.

She seemed to break records with every game, changing the annals of history with her incredible on-court exploits.

Caitlin didn't take long to establish herself on the college scene after coming to Iowa. Her first-year campaign was a scoring clinic, as she scored baskets with a carefree elegance that defied her age. She appeared to soar to new heights with every game, breaking records for the most points scored by a rookie and winning praise from peers and coaches alike.

Caitlin's Record-Breaking Performances

Caitlin's record-breaking achievements only became better as her career developed. She had a level of ability and confidence that made her stand out from her contemporaries, whether she was handing out passes with pinpoint accuracy, making three-pointers from downtown, or driving to the basket with delicacy.

However, there is more to Caitlin's success than simply her skill; it also stems from her relentless work ethic, unshakable perseverance, and enduring enthusiasm for the game.

Future generations of players are inspired to dream big and aim for the stars by her unwavering drive to perfection, which is shown by every record she breaks.

Caitlin's record-breaking accomplishments on the basketball court serve as a constant reminder of the unbounded potential that everyone of us has.

She has transcended her career as a basketball player to become a symbol of inspiration and hope for anybody who has the courage to follow their aspirations thanks to her limitless skill and unwavering determination.

Clark's Unmatched Prowess

The current national player of the year, Caitlin Clark, once again showed her extraordinary abilities throughout the match.

She scored a scorching 38 points, pulled down 10 rebounds, sent out six assists, and committed two steals. During the game, she made 8 out of 15 3-pointers with precision, which further cemented her status as a potent scorer.

A Second-Half Surge

Towards the end of the game, Caitlin Clark showed off her remarkable abilities by scoring 28 points by herself. She credited more passion, pride, and intensity for her outstanding performance in a post-game interview with the Big Ten Network.

In addition, Clark praised the team's overall performance, praising Iowa's efficient ball movement that led to 20 assists.

- **Nearing a Significant Historical Event**:

After putting on a spectacular show of talent, Caitlin Clark is only five points away from being the first female NCAA player to break Jackie Stiles' lifetime scoring record.

This next feat will solidify her incredible career even further and establish her as one of the most prolific scorers in women's collegiate basketball.

- **Team Cohesion Wins:**

The victory versus Nebraska demonstrated the team's collective resiliency in addition to highlighting Caitlin Clark's individual brilliance.

In addition to Clark's outstanding play, Kate Martin scored 16 points, while Sydney Affolter scored 12 points off the bench. In addition to an outstanding 20 assists, the team's effectiveness from 3-point range, which included eight from Clark herself, demonstrated their well-rounded and cohesive style of play.

Chapter 10: Impact Beyond Basketball

Caitlin's Influence and Advocacy

Outside of the basketball court, Caitlin Clark's effect can be felt in the fields of activism and female emancipation, where her voice has a meaningful and purposeful resonance.

Caitlin understands the platform that has been given to her and the responsibility that accompanies it as a well-known person in women's athletics.

She enthusiastically supports efforts to level the playing field and provide ambitious young athletes opportunity by using her prominence to fight for gender equality in sports.

Caitlin encourages a new generation of females to follow their aspirations boldly, shattering preconceptions and obstacles in the process via her words and deeds.

She relentlessly advocates for the value of inclusivity, diversity, and representation in athletics via speaking engagements, social media platforms, and community outreach initiatives.

In addition to gender equality, Caitlin advocates for a number of social topics that are important to her. She utilizes her platform to bring attention to important topics, igniting meaningful debates and promoting good change.

Her advocacy work has ranged from supporting programmes fighting social injustice to promoting mental health awareness.

Caitlin regularly participates in her community in addition to her advocacy work because she understands the value of relationships and giving back. She stays rooted in her heritage, exemplifying the virtues of humility and service, whether she is working at neighborhood youth clinics, inspiring children in classrooms, or taking part in philanthropic activities.

Beyond the boundaries of her sporting accomplishments, Caitlin's activism and influence have a lasting impression on the globe.

Her persistent dedication to empowering people and bringing about change acts as a light of hope and inspiration for future generations as she continues to make progress on and off the court.

Personal Life

Brent Clark, Caitlin Clark's father, is a sales executive at Concentric International and was a player at Simpson College for baseball and basketball. Conversely, her mother, Anne Nizzi-Clark, is of Italian heritage and was once employed as a marketing professional.

She is also the daughter of Bob Nizzi, the renowned former football coach at Dowling Catholic High School.

With an older brother called Blake who played collegiate football at Iowa State and a younger brother named Colin, Caitlin hails from a close-knit family. In addition, Audrey Faber, her cousin, created a name for herself as a Creighton basketball player.

Caitlin's family has a long history of athleticism; two of her uncles were standout athletes in college. Mike Nizzi established his football career at Nebraska–Omaha, while Tom Faber displayed his skills on the court for Drake and Utica.

Outside of her family, Caitlin is in a love relationship with Connor McCaffery, a fellow athlete who excelled at Iowa in baseball and basketball. Connor is notable since he is the son of Fran McCaffery, the men's basketball head coach at the University of Iowa.

In addition to her impressive accomplishments on the basketball court, Caitlin is a dedicated student at the University of Iowa, where she is majoring in marketing. Her selection as a first-team Division I Academic All-American during her sophomore year—a distinguished accolade granted by the College Sports Communicators (CSC)—demonstrates her dedication to greatness beyond sports.

Caitlin's academic excellence was also recognized in 2023 when she was awarded the Division I Women's Basketball Academic All-American of the Year. She went on to receive this honor in all Division I sports.

In addition to her interests in basketball and education, Caitlin has been a passionate golfer since she was a little girl. She got to play with professional golfers Zach Johnson and Ludvig Åberg in the John Deere Classic Pro-Am at

TPC Deere Run in July 2023, demonstrating her ability outside the basketball court.

Enterprises

Excel Sports Management's Alan Zucker, Colleen Garrity, and Erin Kane are Caitlin Clark's representatives.

Analysts have acknowledged her as one of the most marketable athletes and college basketball players, and she has pursued a number of commercial ventures.

Clark signed her first name, image, and likeness (NIL) contract with The Vinyl Studio, a respectable business with headquarters in West Des Moines, Iowa, on August 18, 2021.

She later established a deal with Nike on October 10, 2022, a brand she often wore, especially when it came to sneakers from the Kobe Bryant signature line.

On October 10, 2023, Clark made history by signing a contract with State Farm to serve as their ambassador. He was the first collegiate athlete to do so.

Soon after, she joined forces with Gatorade to increase the number of sponsorships she had, becoming one of the few female basketball players to do so, with Paige Bueckers.

Remarkably, Gatorade honored the partnership by contributing $22,000 to the Caitlin Clark Foundation, which honors her jersey number of 22 and works to improve communities and kids via sports, education, and good nutrition.

In order to broaden her product line, Clark collaborated with Hy-Vee, an Iowa-based grocery company, which in January 2024 will introduce "Caitlin's Crunch Time," a limited-edition cereal. Sales of cereal will generate funds for Clark's charity.

Beyond these endeavors, Clark has also landed NIL partnerships with well-known businesses, demonstrating her diverse presence in the business world.

These firms include Bose, Buick, Goldman Sachs, H&R Block, and Topps, among others.

In pop culture

Caitlin Clark's impact and presence have been recognized in public in a number of ways outside of basketball:

She was honored to toss the ceremonial first pitch for the Iowa Cubs, the Chicago Cubs' Triple-A club, whom she had passionately followed her whole life, in June 2022.

On August 23, of the same year, she repeated the gesture in support of the big league Chicago Cubs, demonstrating her loyalty to the club. The Iowa Cubs honored Caitlin with a bobblehead night as a thank you, highlighting her influence on the community's sports culture.

Caitlin is an avid sports lover, especially football, specifically the Kansas City Chiefs.

Her enthusiasm inspired her to become the first collegiate athlete to host the ManningCast, which she did on November 20, 2023, during a Monday Night Football game against the Chiefs.

When the Iowa State Fair presented a magnificent homage to Caitlin in the shape of a life-size butter sculpture in August 2023, her notoriety skyrocketed.

Her role as a local legend was honored by this prestigious accolade, which put her with notable Iowa collegiate players like Kurt Warner and Jack Trice.

Caitlin's broad popularity was shown in January 2024, when she was the talk of the political world before the Iowa Republican presidential caucuses.

A local audience was present when Nikki Haley, the presidential contender, mistakenly called her "Caitlin Collins" at this period.

Funny rumors circulated about the mix-up, with some linking the mishap to uncertainty about CNN anchor Kaitlan Collins.

When Kaitlan Collins subsequently got a Caitlin Clark jersey from Ron DeSantis, a different presidential contender, during an interview in Iowa, jokingly noting the prior blunder, this affair took a humorous turn.

Chapter 11: The Next Chapter

Caitlin's Ambitions and Goals

Caitlin Clark's aspirations and objectives act as beacons of light, directing her on a path characterized by tenacity, tenacity, and unyielding resolve.

Caitlin's drive to be the best at what she does and have a long-lasting influence on the basketball world is at the core of her goals. She aspires to perfection with every dribble, pass, and shoot, challenging herself to reach new heights and raising the bar with each triumph.

Caitlin's ambition is driven by her unwavering pursuit of achievement, both on her own and as a member of a team. Her aspirations include lifting championship trophies, breaking down nets, and becoming one of the best competitors in basketball history.

Nevertheless, Caitlin's goals go well beyond the basketball court. She has a clear vision for the future and wants to use her position to change the world for the better via activism, charity, or mentoring.

Caitlin is unwavering in her dedication to personal improvement as she keeps improving her abilities and raising her game.

She is aware that there may be difficulties along the way to greatness, but she views every setback as a chance to improve herself as a person and as an athlete.

Chapter 12: Legacy in Motion

Caitlin's Enduring Impact on the Sport

The long-lasting influence of Caitlin Clark on basketball is diverse and extends beyond the game itself. The following are some essential components that contribute to her enduring influence:

Scoring Prowess:

Caitlin is one of the game's most exciting scorers due to her ability to rack up scores in large quantities.

She has completely changed the definition of what it means to be a scoring danger on the court because of her lethal mix of long shooting range, superb ball handling abilities, and a talent for constructing her own shots.

Playmaking Skills:

In addition to her ability to score, Caitlin has excellent court vision and a sharp basketball IQ, which combine to make her a powerful playmaker who improves the performance of her teammates. She is a triple threat on offense because of her ability to thread the needle with precise passes and create scoring chances for others.

Leadership Qualities:

Caitlin inspires those around her with her work ethic, enthusiasm, and devotion to the game. She is a natural leader both on and off the court.

Her leadership presence creates a lasting impression on everyone she comes into contact with, whether it's encouraging her teammates at a critical time in a game or acting as an inspiration for ambitious young athletes.

Impact on Women's Basketball:

Caitlin's ascent to fame has highlighted the skill and athleticism of female players while drawing fresh attention to women's basketball. Her national fame and talent demonstrate the popularity of women's sports and encourage a new generation of girls to follow their aspirations on the court.

Off-Court Influence:

In addition to her accomplishments on the court, Caitlin utilizes her position to support social justice and gender equality in athletics. She increases her influence and shows that athletes have the ability to positively affect society via her advocacy.

All things considered, Caitlin Clark's lasting influence on basketball can be attributed to her extraordinary skill, her capacity for leadership, and her dedication to changing the game both on and off the court.

Her legacy will motivate and inspire players for many decades to come as she develops both as a player and as a person.

Media Attention:

Caitlin's exciting play style and outstanding performances have attracted a lot of media attention, which has increased the number of people watching women's basketball games and attracted new followers to the sport.

Her appearance in news articles, highlight videos, and social media posts encourages a wider audience to become aware of and interested in the sport.

Youth Inspiration:

Caitlin's accomplishments serve as an inspiration and motivational factor for aspiring basketball players throughout the globe, positioning her as a role model for young athletes.

Her transformation from a small-town athlete to a college star shows that anything is achievable with perseverance, hard effort, and devotion.

Commercial Opportunities:

Caitlin's marketability and popularity make her a valuable commercial asset for women's basketball overall as well as for herself. Her celebrity power draws attention from businesses looking to identify themselves with her good image and impact, leading to endorsement partnerships and sponsorship agreements.

Record-Breaking Performances:

Caitlin has broken several records and accomplished incredible feats over her career, solidifying her status as one of the greatest players in women's basketball history. Her accomplishments leave an enduring impression on the record books and set standards for next generations of athletes to strive for and exceed.

Global Reach:

Caitlin's influence transcends national boundaries, engaging viewers from across the world and demonstrating the skill and competitiveness of women's basketball worldwide.

She raises the standard of play and the sport's visibility globally as she plays against elite athletes from across the globe.

Educational options:

Caitlin's athletic accomplishments provide her and other ambitious student-athletes access to academic programs and scholarships, among other educational options.

She exemplifies academic brilliance and highlights the need of a well-rounded education by doing very well in both the classroom and on the court.

Long-Term Legacy:

Caitlin will leave a lasting legacy that goes far beyond her playing days as her career develops and her influence on the sport only increases. She will go on influencing women's basketball and motivating future generations of players via her coaching, mentoring, and advocacy activities.

Career Highlights and Awards

- Big Ten Freshman of the Year:

Given to her during her first season as a Hawkeye.

- NCAA Women's Basketball Tournament All-Region Team:

Acknowledgment for exceptional NCAA Tournament performance.

- All-Big Ten First Team:

Awarded for superior conference performance.

- Finalist for the Nancy Lieberman Award:

Awarded to the best point guard in women's college basketball.

- ESPNW National Player of the Week:

Honored for outstanding contributions made during the campaign.

- Big Ten Player of the Week:

Awarded several times for exceptional conference play efforts.

- Naismith Trophy Watch List:

Selected for the esteemed Naismith Trophy, which is given to the best college basketball player.

- John R. Wooden Award Watch List:

Added to the list of nominees for the John R. Wooden Award, which honors the best college basketball player.

- Associated Press All-America First Team:

Named to the Associated Press's "Top Team" of players in the country.

- USA Today All-America First Team:

Selected for exceptional achievement to the esteemed USA Today All-America First Team.

Conclusion

"In Search of Greatness: The Caitlin Clark Biography" has given readers a close-up look at Caitlin Clark's incredible journey, which is motivated by an unquenchable desire for greatness on and off the basketball court.

Readers have watched Caitlin's unyielding dedication to her art, her ceaseless quest of excellence, and her unflinching resolve to make a lasting impression on the sports world via the pages of this book.

One pattern becomes evident when we consider Caitlin's incredible story: striving for greatness is a very personal path of self-actualization and self-discovery rather than just seeking recognition or affirmation from others.

Caitlin's unshakable commitment to her sport goes beyond just trying to win or get recognition; it also involves her constant pursuit of improving as a person and an athlete.

Throughout her path, Caitlin has shown the virtues of tenacity, fortitude, and honesty; she has faced hardship with dignity and humility and has turned setbacks into chances for personal development.

Her steadfast devotion to her objectives, her unflinching confidence in herself, and her rigorous work ethic serve as an example to those who strive for excellence, both in and outside of the athletics world.

In the end, "In Search of Greatness" is a tribute to the strength of desire, tenacity, and purpose rather than just the life story of a basketball prodigy. It serves as a reminder that everyone who is prepared to give their all to their goals may achieve greatness and is not only reserved for a select few.

We can only speculate as to the heights Caitlin may achieve and the effects she will have on the globe as she continues on her quest.

One thing is for sure, though: her desire for both athletic and personal excellence will serve as a source of inspiration for future generations, encouraging each of us to strive for greatness in our own lives.